DISCARDED

Milton-Union Public Library
West Milton. Ohio

APR 1

APR 16

DEER HUNTING

by Tom Carpenter

Content Consultant
Bill Sherck
Outdoor Television Show Host

Milton Union Public Library
West Milton, Ohio

SportsZone

An Imprint of Abdo Publishing
abdopublishing.com

abdopublishing.com

Published by Abdo Publishing, a division of ABDO, PO Box 398166, Minneapolis, Minnesota 55439. Copyright © 2016 by Abdo Consulting Group, Inc. International copyrights reserved in all countries. No part of this book may be reproduced in any form without written permission from the publisher. SportsZone™ is a trademark and logo of Abdo Publishing.

Printed in the United States of America, North Mankato, Minnesota
042015
092015

THIS BOOK CONTAINS RECYCLED MATERIALS

Cover Photos: Scott Bolster/Shutterstock Images (background); Paul Tessier/Shutterstock Images (foreground)
Interior Photos: Scott Bolster/Shutterstock Images, 1 (background); Paul Tessier/Shutterstock Images, 1 (foreground); Makoto Hori/Kyodo/AP Images, 4–5; Bruce MacQueen/Shutterstock Images, 6; Shutterstock Images, 10–11, 30–31; Paul Tessier/iStockphoto, 12, 22; Frank Hilderbrand/iStockphoto, 14; Michael DeFreitas/Danita Delimont Photography/Newscom, 17; Laura May/Oshkosh Northwestern/AP Images, 20–21; Brent Frazee/MCT/Newscom, 24; Jeff Vanuga/Corbis, 27; Dale Spartas/Corbis, 28; William Albert Allard/National Geographic, 33; Patrick Pleul/DPA/AP Images, 34; Sue Beyer/The Express-Times/AP Images, 37; Wayne Hughes/Alamy, 38–39; Derek Montgomery/MCT/Newscom, 40–41; Guy Cali Stock Connection Worldwide/Newscom, 42; Bob DeMay/Akron Beacon Journal/AP Images, 44

Editor: Jon Westmark
Series Designer: Jake Nordby

Library of Congress Control Number: 2015931668

Cataloging-in-Publication Data
Carpenter, Tom.
 Deer hunting / Tom Carpenter.
   p. cm. -- (Hunting)
Includes bibliographical references and index.
ISBN 978-1-62403-833-4
1. Deer hunting--Juvenile literature.   I. Title.
799.2/765--dc23

                                                    2015931668

CONTENTS

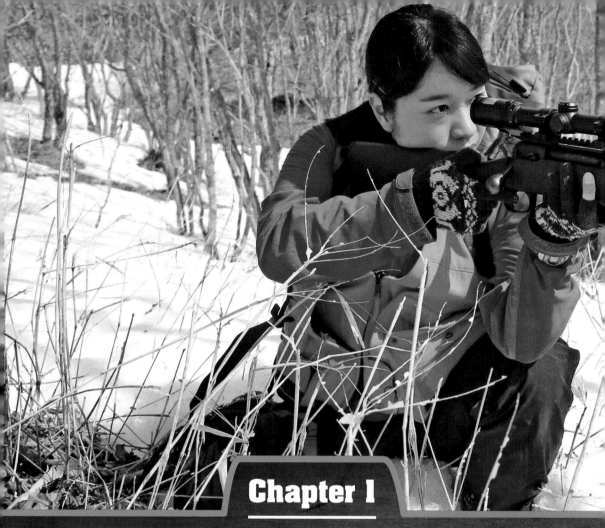

Chapter 1

WELCOME TO DEER HUNTING

On a sunny late-November afternoon, a young woman stands with her brother and father on a snowy ridgetop, talking softly.

Hunters often kneel or lie down to use the ground to help support their shots.

Soon their plan is set. The young woman walks a long loop through fields and across pastures. She enters a wooded area, goes down a steep hillside, and sits near the bottom, where the forest meets a marsh.

Deer often use the same trails. But if they sense danger, they may use different routes.

Three deer trails come together here. The woman's family will walk through the forest toward her and try to get a deer to move in her direction.

Her brother and father spread out across the forested hillside. They begin walking toward the waiting shooter. They walk slowly, pausing often to spook any deer hiding in the brush. The hunters push through thickets, where deer like to hide.

The hunters know where the young woman is waiting. They will not shoot in her direction.

The woman watches the woods ahead—fifteen minutes, twenty minutes, a half hour. The warm sun makes her a little sleepy. But then, shuffling leaves and a cracking twig alert her. She rises slowly to one knee.

A buck! The male whitetail runs off the hillside, turns left, and runs straight toward her. Then the buck switches trails. It slows and passes only 30 yards (27 m) away. It pauses to smell the breeze. The woman aims her rifle.

Boom! The buck jumps and runs off with the shot. The young woman's family arrives. Together they find some deer hair and follow sprays of blood along the trail. Soon they spot the deer ahead—a buck stretched out in the leaves!

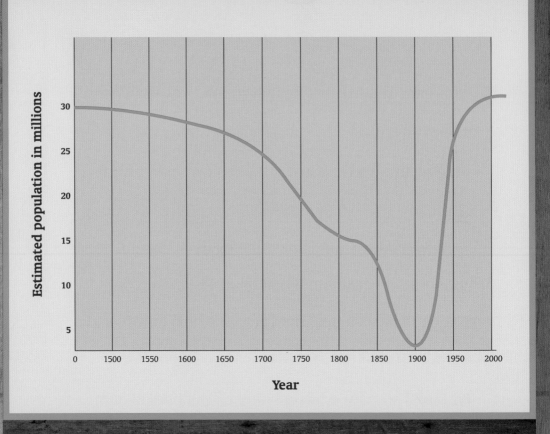

The white-tailed deer population dropped to an estimated 500,000 in the United States in 1900. Hunting rules have helped whitetail numbers rebound.

The young woman walks over and makes sure the whitetail is dead. Her heart is still beating quickly. She cannot believe she just shot her first buck. She proudly holds the deer's seven-point rack in her hands. Her family congratulates her.

Deer Hunting History

Deer hunting has a long history in North America. Native Americans used longbows to hunt deer for food. They used every part of a harvested deer including the skin.

But deer populations soon decreased when Europeans arrived in North America. The settlers did not set hunting seasons or regulations. In many places, deer were completely killed off.

By the early 1900s, game managers started setting hunting seasons and whitetail harvest limits. Deer populations recovered.

Today deer hunting is one of the most popular outdoor activities in North America. Millions of deer are harvested each year in the United States, Canada, and Mexico.

Hunters pursue deer alone or in groups. Some hunt in tree stands. Others hunt on the ground. People use rifles, shotguns, and bows to hunt deer. But no matter how it is done, deer hunting is an exciting and challenging sport.

Chapter 2

BIOLOGY AND HABITAT

Deer are challenging to hunt. They have finely
tuned senses that allow them to detect danger.
Deer hunters must understand the traits, habits,
and habitat of their prey to be successful.

Deer can identify up to six different smells at once.

White-tailed deer and mule deer are the two main types of deer hunted in North America.

White-Tailed Deer

White-tailed deer thrive in many kinds of habitats across the United States, southern

11

Whitetails often flick or twitch their bright tails. This can help hunters notice them at long distances.

Canada, and Mexico. In the north, mature bucks weigh from 150 to 200 pounds (68–91 kg). Does weigh from 100 to 125 pounds (45–57 kg). Deer are larger in the north to better fight winter snow and cold. In the south, deer are smaller. Bucks weigh 125 to 175 pounds (57–79 kg), and does weigh 75 to 100 pounds (34–45 kg).

Whitetails have reddish-colored coats in summer that change to gray-brown in winter. Whitetails are named after their wide tails with bright white undersides. Deer flash these tails and run when danger is near. This is called flagging. It alerts other deer of the threat. It also tells predators that it is time to give up because the deer has spotted or smelled them.

White-tailed deer have an incredible sense of smell. Their noses can detect a human a half-mile (0.8 km) or more away. Deer hear very well too, so hunters must be quiet. Whitetails have good sight, but it is based on motion. Even a hunter in blaze orange may escape being seen if the hunter sits very still.

Whitetails are extremely adaptable. They live in many kinds of habitats, including farmland, deep wilderness, hill country, swamps, marshes, and even suburban areas.

Bucks use trees and branches to clean the velvet from their antlers. Hunters can look for trees missing bark when scouting.

Whitetails browse when they feed. They eat a variety of food while on the move. Deer often eat farm crops such as alfalfa, corn, soybeans, and wheat. In the wilderness, they eat buds, leaves, and grasses.

White-tailed deer breed from October through December. The peak is in early November. This breeding season is known as the rut. Fawns are born in May and June. They stay with their mother for a year, until she has new fawns.

Whitetail bucks grow new antlers every year. The antlers start to grow in spring. At first they are covered with velvet—a soft, thick skin full of blood vessels. The antlers harden in September, and bucks rub their antlers on trees and branches to help clean off the velvet. Antlers help a buck compete with other bucks for does during the rut. Antlers drop off in late winter.

Humans often change deer habitat through farming, building, logging, and other activities. But whitetails are good at adapting. Whitetails are also good at avoiding hunters. Sometimes whitetails overpopulate their habitat. Hunting seasons can trim deer populations so the herd stays healthy and every animal has enough to eat.

Mule Deer

Mule deer—also called muleys—live in the western United States and Canada. They are named for their ears, which are big like a mule's. Mule deer have reddish-gray coats in the summer and pure gray coats in the winter. Mule deer bucks are big. Mature bucks weigh from 175 to 250 pounds (79–113 kg). Does weigh 100 to 150 pounds (45–68 kg). Muley bucks' antlers are often wide and tall. Bucks shed their antlers each year.

Muleys are stocky and muscular. Their tails are short and rope-like and white with a black tip. Mule deer have an interesting way of moving, called stotting. They spring into the air with each stride, keeping their legs close together. The motion is good for climbing hills, hopping over obstacles, and escaping predators.

Western foothills, mountains, prairies, and deserts provide good habitat for mule deer. They live in big,

Stotting mule deer can be difficult to shoot. It's best to shoot deer that are stopped or moving slowly.

wide-open spaces where they can see danger from far away.

Mule deer have an excellent sense of smell. They sneak away from areas at the first hint of dangerous scents. Muley hearing is also very good. Their big ears can turn to pinpoint sounds. Mule deer eyesight is good too. They can spot slight movement from more than 1,900 feet (580 m) away.

Most mule deer live in wild places, where they feed on shrubs such as sage and mountain mahogany. They also feed on forbs and grasses. Mule deer feed in farm and ranch fields when they can. Irrigated hayfields really attract mule deer.

Breeding season is later for mule deer than whitetails. The rut peaks in late November. Mule deer have their fawns in late May and June. At this time, does live near creeks and springs where there is plenty to drink and eat.

As humans populate more of western

Black-Tailed Deer

Black-tailed deer live along the West Coast—from northern California through Oregon, Washington, and British Columbia to Alaska. Blacktails are technically the same species as mule deer. The two have similar ears. But blacktails have tails similar in size to those of whitetails. Blacktails live in dense woods and thickets. They tend to be smaller than mule deer and whitetails.

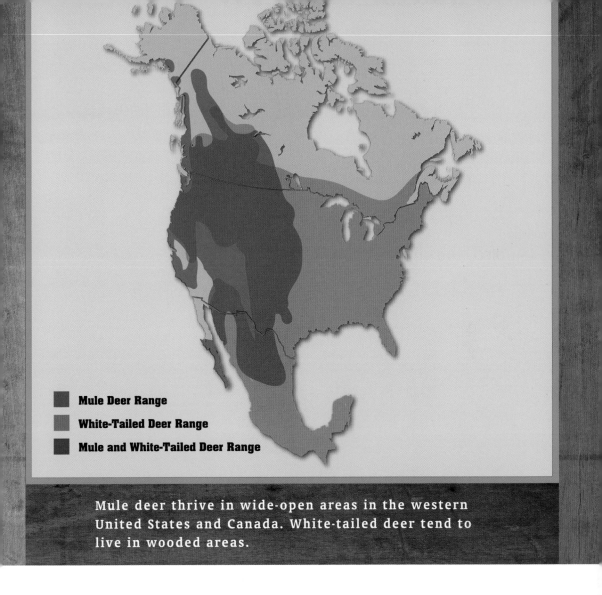

Mule deer thrive in wide-open areas in the western United States and Canada. White-tailed deer tend to live in wooded areas.

North America, mule deer are pushed farther into the remaining wilderness. Game managers often have to limit the number of mule deer hunting licenses given out so the deer do not become overhunted.

Chapter 3

TECHNIQUES

A successful deer hunter is patient, quiet, and focused on the hunt. Good hunters also go into the field with a specific plan in mind. Wandering

Hunters must be patient and watchful to see deer.

through deer habitat and hoping to find a deer to shoot will not produce good results.

Scouting

Successful deer hunting starts with scouting. Scouting reveals where deer are feeding,

Game cameras give hunters important information about where and when animals pass by.

bedding, and watering. Hunters can also find the trails deer use to get from one location to another.

Hunters should get out before deer hunting season to look for deer tracks, droppings, paths, rubs, and scrapes.

Rubs and scrapes are territory markers that bucks make. It is best to scout at midday, when deer are hiding in deep cover. Deer are not as disturbed by human actions at this time.

In open areas, hunters can scout by sitting on a hill with binoculars at dawn or dusk. They can watch for deer and take note of where the animals are moving and feeding.

Game cameras are also important scouting tools. Many serious hunters put a few up to take pictures of deer roaming the hunting grounds. Scouting cameras also reveal when and where deer are moving.

Stand Hunting

Many deer hunters stand hunt. Stand hunting means the hunter stays still and waits for a deer to appear. A good spot for a stand is along a trail between deer bedding and feeding areas. Another good place is in an area where deer travel to avoid other hunters.

A tree stand helps a hunter stay out of sight.

Many stand hunters wait above the ground in tree stands. Some use ground blinds. Others wait next to a tree or log.

There are a few simple but important keys to successful stand hunting. It is important to set the stand up so the wind blows from the deer trail or feeding area to the hunter. Hunters must wait quietly and make as little movement as possible when stand hunting. Otherwise the deer will notice them. Successful hunters pay attention and spot deer long before they are close.

Still Hunting

Still hunting does not mean that hunters stand completely still. Instead hunters move slowly along. They move so slowly, it almost seems like they are standing still. The hunter stops and waits often, to study the landscape and look for deer.

Still hunting is best in woods and thickets where deer may be moving around during the daytime. Hunters

Deer Spotting Secrets

It can be hard to see deer in thick forests and brush. Deer may blend in well with their surroundings. Or only a portion of a deer may be visible. Hunters look for the horizontal lines of a deer's back or belly. They also look for the flick of a tail or twitch of an ear.

should move as slowly as possible—only a few steps at a time. They should walk into the wind so deer in front of them cannot smell them easily. The best still hunters pause near trees to break up their outline. They watch and look for longer than they move.

Spot-and-Stalk Hunting

In open environments, spotting and stalking is an effective approach. Hunters set up in a place where they can see a lot of land. But they stay below the top of ridges or hills. This way, deer below will not see their shape against the sky. Spot-and-stalk hunters use binoculars and spotting scopes to look for deer to stalk.

Spot-and-stalk hunters hunt in big, open areas.

The next step is planning the stalk. A good route keeps the hunter hidden behind terrain and vegetation on the way toward the deer. A good stalk route also keeps the hunter's scent from blowing to the deer. Spot-and-stalk hunters sneak into shooting range of a deer for a good shot.

Snow allows hunters to see deer tracks more clearly. This can make deer easier to follow.

Pushing Deer

Sometimes hunters get together to hunt deer. Some

people call this a deer drive. But deer are not really driven.

They go where they want to go. Other people call this method pushing deer.

When pushing deer, hunters spread out and walk through an area. One or more hunters go to spots where deer may travel after being disturbed by the other hunters. The standing hunters, or posters, wait quietly. The walking hunters, or pushers, must walk through thick areas to get deer up and moving.

Safety is an especially important consideration when pushing deer. Posters should not shoot toward each other or the line of pushers. Pushers should never shoot in the direction of the posters or other pushers.

Tracking

Some hunters try to track deer when it snows during hunting season. These hunters walk woodland lanes or roads early in the morning after a fresh snowfall. They look for deer tracks. Then the hunters follow the tracks. They move quickly at first to catch up. Then they slow down to look for the deer.

Chapter 4

EQUIPMENT AND SKILLS

The most important piece of hunting equipment is the firearm or bow the hunter uses to shoot the deer. Many hunters use rifles. Rifles can kill a deer from up to 300 yards (274 m) away. But

Bolt-action rifles allow hunters to quickly and reliably cycle through cartridges.

shots from 150 or 200 yards (137 or 183 m) are more effective. In open areas, bolt-action rifles are popular because of their extreme accuracy for the longer-range shots. In woods and brushy areas, some hunters prefer lever-action or semiautomatic rifles for quick follow-up shots.

In some places, shotguns loaded with rifled slugs work best. These slugs are bigger than rifle bullets. They do not travel as far. Slugs are safer in areas where there are farms and livestock around. Modern shotguns can shoot slugs accurately up to 100 or 125 yards (91 or 114 m).

Many states offer special seasons for hunters using muzzle-loading rifles. Muzzle-loaders are old-fashioned rifles. Hunters load these guns by pushing the powder and bullet down the barrel from the open end. Muzzle-loaders make the hunt more challenging. They can only shoot once before they need to be reloaded. But not all muzzle-loaders are old. Many are modern, high-tech guns. These can be accurate out to 150 yards (137 m) or more.

Bowhunting is another challenging way to hunt deer. Most bows and arrows limit the hunter's shooting distance to approximately 30 yards (27 m). Crossbows are deadly

In recent years, more states have begun to allow crossbow hunting.

from 40 to 50 yards (37–46 m) and are becoming more popular for deer hunting.

Many hunters hunt deer from tree stands. Tree stands get the hunter above the deer. This offers a better view

Deer hunters often clear away brush and tree branches before the season starts. This allows them to see certain areas clearly from their stands.

for the hunter and may keep some scent away from the deer's nose.

One of the best tree stands is a ladder stand. This stand allows hunters to climb easily up to a platform. They sit on a seat on the platform to hunt. Some people try to make their own tree stands using wood and nails. These types of stands are unreliable and can be dangerous. Hunters should use only stands approved by the Treestand Manufacturer's Association.

Good optics help hunters spot deer in the woods and in open areas. Eight- to 10-power, full-sized binoculars are just right for deer hunting. Range finders help hunters identify the distance to a deer or to certain objects. Knowing distances is an important part of making good shots. Spotting scopes are good in the mountains. They help hunters look for deer that are very far away.

Deer hunters need to dress properly for the hunt. Most hunters dress in layers. Layers trap warm air between them. They also allow hunters to remove clothing if they become too warm. Some hunters wear scent-blocking clothing. This helps keep the deer from picking up a hunter's scent.

A deer hunter needs good boots. Hunters who move a lot, such as in spot-and-stalk hunting, need comfortable boots for hiking. Stand hunters need boots that will keep their feet warm while they sit for long periods of time.

A good knife is important to field dress an animal. Both folding knives and fixed-blade knives do the job.

Deer Hunting Skills

Good deer hunters understand how a deer's superior senses work. To go undetected, hunters hunt into the wind. They stay still and quiet when they are in a stand, moving only when they need to.

Another important skill is shooting. One key for good shooting is to squeeze the trigger gently. Pulling or jerking the trigger can cause the gun to move away from the target. Serious deer hunters practice with their firearms or bows before the season. They become accurate and confident shooting their weapons. They do not want to miss their chances when deer appear.

Tracking in pairs allows one person to follow the blood trail and the other to keep an eye out for the wounded deer.

Deer do not always fall down on the spot when hunters hit them with a shot. This is especially the case when bowhunting. Hunters often need to follow a blood trail to find the deer. It is best to do this in pairs. One person follows the blood trail. The other watches ahead for the deer, ready to shoot again if it gets up.

MAKING THE SHOT

Blaze Orange: Blaze orange helps hunters see one another.

Rest: Rests help hunters keep their guns steady for accurate shooting.

Scope: High-power scopes help hunters place their shots.

Tree Stand: Tree stands allow hunters to get above deer and go unnoticed.

Chapter 5

SAFETY AND CONSERVATION

Deer hunters must follow certain guidelines to have a safe and legal experience. Most states and provinces require hunters to wear blaze orange during firearm hunting seasons. Blaze

Blaze orange is easy for humans to see from long distances. But the color does not stand out to deer.

orange clothing helps hunters see one another so they know where it is safe to shoot.

As with all kinds of hunting, deer hunters must follow firearm safety rules. It can be easy to get excited when a deer is close by. This is

Practicing at a firing range helps hunters become comfortable and safe with their firearms.

called buck fever. But no deer is worth the risk of shooting someone else or damaging property. All hunters should take a firearm safety course to learn how to handle their guns safely and effectively.

Hunters also need to plan what they will do with the deer after it is harvested. It is against the law to waste deer meat. Processing the meat starts with field dressing the animal. Field dressing allows meat to cool and stay fresh until it can be butchered.

Licensing and Conservation

Deer hunters must have the proper hunting license for the state or province in which they are hunting. The money generated from

TAB-K Formula

One good way to remember how to be safe with a firearm is by following the TAB-K formula:

T— Treat every firearm as if it were loaded at all times.

A— Always point the barrel of the gun in a safe direction.

B— Be certain of your target and what's beyond it.

K— Keep your finger outside of the trigger guard until you are ready to shoot.

Youth hunts give young people an opportunity to gain experience without competing against adult hunters.

selling hunting licenses helps game departments manage species of all kinds. Hunters should follow all rules as outlined in the game department's official regulations booklet. That booklet might be printed, available online, or both.

Hunters play an important role in conservation. Deer hunting can help keep populations from overrunning their habitats. Hunters act as predators, removing some deer so the rest stay healthy and have enough to eat.

Many states hold antlerless deer hunts in which does can be taken. This helps reduce deer populations because it limits the number of deer born the next spring. Special youth hunts are also available in many places, so kids have days of their own to learn the sport of deer hunting with a family member or other experienced hunter.

Deer Hunting Trophies

Shooting a deer is a big accomplishment. Hunters honor the memory of the hunt, and a great animal, in many ways. Some mount antlers on plaques. Others have a full shoulder mount created with their trophy buck. Tanned skins also make nice trophies. And snapping pictures is a great way to capture the memory of any special hunting trip.

GLOSSARY

blind
A portable, tent-like structure that a hunter can set up on the ground to hide from game.

bolt-action rifle
A firearm with a hand-operated action that is pulled up and back to eject a cartridge and pushed forward and down to load a new one.

buckshot
Large pellets, also known as shot or BBs, in a shotgun shell. Buckshot is only effective at close ranges.

field dress
The process of removing organs and intestines from a dead deer so that the meat cools quickly.

forbs
Flowering plants. Deer often eat forbs.

lever-action rifle
A firearm that uses a lever to load cartridges into the chamber.

optics
Binoculars and spotting scopes used to spot, watch, and study game.

range finder
Optics that allow a hunter to measure the distance to a target.

rifled slug
A single bullet or projectile that is fired from a shotgun.

semiautomatic rifle
A firearm that automatically ejects used cartridges and inserts new ones from a clip.

FOR MORE INFORMATION

Further Reading

Graubart, Norman D. *How to Track a Deer.* New York: Windmill Books, 2015.

Llanas, Sheila Griffin. *White-Tailed Deer.* Minneapolis: Abdo Publishing, 2014.

Pound, Blake. *Deer Hunting.* Minneapolis: Bellwether Media, Inc., 2013.

Websites

To learn more about Hunting, visit **booklinks.abdopublishing.com**. These links are routinely monitored and updated to provide the most current information available.

INDEX

ABOUT THE AUTHOR

Tom Carpenter is a father, a sportsman, and an outdoor writer. He has introduced many children, including his three sons, to the thrills and rewards of hunting. A native son of Wisconsin who always has part of his heart in South Dakota, he planted roots in the middle. He lives with his family near the shores of Bass Lake, Minnesota.